Learn to Crochet Circles into Squares

Taking a circle and making it into a square is a unique variation on the basic granny square. Once you follow the step-by-step instructions you will be able to accomplish any of the projects in this book. So take your pick, from dishcloths to afghans, a scarf or perhaps a pillow, and enjoy.

6

8

10

14

17

20

22

26

LEISURE ARTS, INC. • Maumelle, Arkansas

How to Make a Circle into a Square

Follow these easy instructions to make a simple circle into a square motif that can be used in a variety of projects. Starting with a basic circle you will work your way around and increase the stitches until you have the piece big enough to make the square. Making the transition from the circle to the square is simply a matter of creating a corner by making longer stitches and then working your way to create the next corner by making smaller and smaller stitches. Just follow the step-by-step instructions and you will be amazed at how easy it is to accomplish.

Step 1
Chain 4.

Step 2
Work 11 double crochet into 4th chain from hook, slip stitch to the top of the beginning chain to join. The first 3 skipped chains will count as a double crochet. (12 double crochet).

Step 3

Chain 3 (counts as double crochet), double crochet in same space, work 2 double crochet in each stitch around, join with a slip stitch to top of chain 3. (24 double crochet)

Step 4

Chain 3, double crochet in same stitch, double crochet in next stitch, (2 double crochet in next stitch, double crochet in next stitch) repeat around, join with slip stitch to the top of the chain 3. Fasten off. (36 double crochet)

Step 5

Join new color with a slip st in any double crochet, chain 3.

Step 6

Double crochet, chain 2, 2 double crochet in same space.

Step 7

Double crochet in next stitch, half double crochet in next 2 stitches, single crochet in the next 2 stitches (this will start to take the circle and make it into a square).

Step 8

Half double crochet in the next 2 stitches and then double crochet in the next.

Step 9

Work 2 double crochet, chain 2, 2 double crochet in the next stitch (this will create the corner). Repeat Steps 7, 8 & 9 around; then slip stitch to the top of the chain 3 to join.

Step 10

Chain 3, double crochet in the next stitch, (2 double crochet, chain 2, 2 double crochet) in the corner chain 2 from last row.

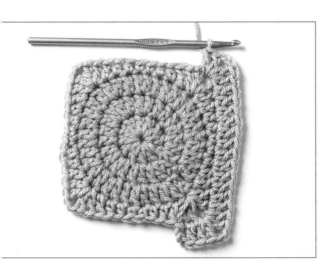

Step 11

Work double crochet in the next 12 stitches and (2 double crochet, chain 2, 2 double crochet) in the corner chain 2.

Repeat Step 11 around the square, ending with a double crochet in each of the last 10 stitches. Join with a slip stitch to the top of the chain 3. Fasten off.

Scarf

SHOPPING LIST

Yarn Worsted Weight 🧶 **MEDIUM 4**
yarn, 100% acrylic, 5 oz/141g
(approx 256 yds/234 m)
- ☐ Color A: 1 Skein Purple
- ☐ Color B: 1 Skein White
- ☐ Color C: 1 Skein Light Grey

Crochet Hook
- ☐ I-9 (5.5 mm) or size needed for gauge

Additional Supplies
- ☐ Yarn needle

SIZE INFORMATION

Size: 6½" x 65" (16.5 cm x 165cm)

GAUGE INFORMATION

One Square = 6½" x 6½" /
16.5 cm x 16.5 cm

Scarf Square

Make 10
With A, ch 4.

Round 1: Work 11 dc in 4th ch from hook, slip st to top of beginning ch to join, (first 3 skipped chs count as dc) – 12 dc.

Round 2: Ch 3 (counts as dc now and throughout), dc in same space, 2 dc in each dc around, slip st to top of beginning ch – 24 dc. Fasten off.

Round 3: Join B with a slip st in any dc, ch 3, dc in same space, dc in next dc, [2 dc in next dc, dc in next dc] around, slip st to top of beginning ch – 36 dc. Fasten off.

Round 4: Join C with a slip st in any dc, ch 3, (dc, ch 2, 2 dc) in same space, *dc in next dc, hdc in next 2 dc, sc in next 2 dc, hdc in next 2 dc, dc in next dc, (2 dc, ch 2, 2 dc) in next dc; repeat from * 3 times, end with dc in next dc, hdc in next 2 dc, sc in next 2 dc, hdc in next 2 dc, dc in next 2 dc, slip st to top of beginning ch.

Round 5: Ch 3, dc in next st, *[2 dc, ch 2, 2 dc] in ch 2 space, {ch 1, skip 1, dc in next st} 5 times, ch 1; repeat from * 3 times, ending last repeat with {ch 1, skip 1, dc in next st} 4 times, ch 1 join with slip st to top of ch 3. Fasten off.

Round 6: Join A with a slip st in last ch 1 space of previous row, ch 3, dc in next 4 sts, *(dc, ch 2, dc) in ch 2 corner, dc in next 15 sts or ch spaces; repeat from * ending with dc in next 11 sts or ch space. Join with slip st. Fasten off.

FINISHING:

Sew Squares together.

Dishcloth

◼◼◻◻ **EASY**

SHOPPING LIST

Yarn Worsted Weight **④** MEDIUM
yarn, 100% cotton, 2½ oz /50g
(approx 125 yds / 115m)

- ☐ Color A: 1 Skein Light Blue
- ☐ Color B: 1 Skein Light Green
- ☐ Color C: 1 Skein White

Crochet Hook

- ☐ I-9 (5.5 mm) or size needed
  for gauge

Additional Supplies

- ☐ Yarn needle

SIZE INFORMATION

Size: 6½" x 6½"/
16.5 cm x 16.5 cm

GAUGE INFORMATION

One Square = 6½" x 6½"/
16.5 cm x 16.5 cm

Dishcloth 1

With A, ch 4.

Round 1: Work 11 dc in 4th ch from hook, slip st to top of beginning ch to join, (first 3 skipped chs count as dc) – 12 dc.

Round 2: Ch 3 (counts as dc now and throughout), dc in same space, 2 dc in each dc around, slip st to top of beginning ch – 24 dc. Fasten off.

Round 3: Join B with a slip st in any dc, ch 3, dc in same space, dc in next dc, [2 dc in next dc, dc in next dc] around, slip st to top of beginning ch – 36 dc. Fasten off.

Round 4: Join C with a slip st in any dc, ch 3, (dc, ch 2, 2 dc) in same space, *dc in next dc, hdc in next 2 dc, sc in next 2 dc, hdc in next 2 dc, dc in next dc, (2 dc, ch 2, 2 dc) in next dc; repeat from * 3 times, end with dc in next dc, hdc in next 2 dc, sc in next 2 dc, hdc in next 2 dc, dc in next 2 dc, slip st to top of beginning ch. Fasten off.

Round 5: Join A with a slip st in last st of previous round, ch 3, dc in the next 3 dc, (2 dc, ch 2, 2 dc) in ch 2 space, *dc in next 12 dc, (2 dc, ch 2, 2 dc) in the ch 2 space; repeat from * twice more, dc in the next 8 dc, join with a slip st to ch 3. Fasten off.

Round 6: Join B with a slip st in last st of previous round, ch 3, dc in the next dc in the next 5 dc, (dc, ch 2, 2 dc) in ch 2 space, *dc in next 16 sts, (2 dc, ch 2, 2 dc) in ch 2 space; repeat from * twice more, dc in next 10 dc, join with slip st to ch 3.

Round 7: Ch 1, sc in same st, sc in next st, ch 3, slip st into first ch of ch 3 (1 picot made), * [sc in next 2 sts, ch3, slip st into first ch of ch 3 (1 picot made)], repeat to corner, (2 sc, make picot, 2 sc, make picot) repeat from * around, join with a slip st to ch 1. Fasten off.

Dishcloth 2

Work the same as Dishcloth 1 only change colors as follows:

Begin with B.

Row 1: B

Row 2: B

Row 3: A

Row 4: C

Row 5: B

Row 6: A

Row 7: A

Dishcloth 1

Dishcloth 2

Placemats

SHOPPING LIST

Yarn Fine Weight
yarn, 100% cotton
(approx 150 yds/ 164 m)
- ☐ Color A: 1 Skein Light Green
- ☐ Color B: 1 Skein Blue
- ☐ Color C: 1 Skein White

Crochet Hook
- ☐ F-4 (4 mm) or size needed
  for gauge

Additional Supplies
- ☐ Yarn needle

SIZE INFORMATION

Size: 10½" x 16½"/
(26.5 cm x 42 cm)

GAUGE INFORMATION

One Square = 5½" x 5½"/
14 cm x 14 cm

Note: The squares may need to be
blocked to achieve correct size.

Square

Make 6

With A, ch 4.

Round 1: Work 11 dc in 4th ch from
hook, slip st to top of beginning ch
to join, (first 3 skipped chs count
as dc) – 12 dc.

Round 2: Ch 3 (counts as dc now
and throughout), dc in same
space, 2 dc in each dc around,
slip st to top of beginning ch –
24 dc. Fasten off.

Round 3: Join B with a slip st in
any dc, ch 3, dc in same space, dc
in next dc, [2 dc in next dc, dc in
next dc] around, slip st to top of
beginning ch – 36 dc. Fasten off.

Round 4: Join C with a slip st in any
dc, ch 3, (dc, ch 2, 2 dc) in same
space, *dc in next dc, hdc in next
2 dc, sc in next 3 dc, hdc in next 2
dc, dc in next dc, (2 dc, ch 2, 2 dc)
in next dc; repeat from * 3 times,
end with dc in next dc, hdc in next
2 dc, sc in next 3 dc, hdc in next 2
dc, dc in next dc, slip st to top of
beginning ch. Fasten off.

Round 5: Join A with a slip st in the
slip st from previous row, ch 3, dc
in next st, *(2 dc, ch 2, 2 dc) in ch-2
space, dc in next 12 sts; repeat
from * 2 times, (2 dc, ch 2, 2 dc) in
ch-2 space, dc in next 10 sts, slip s
to top of beginning ch. Fasten off

Round 6: Join B with a slip st
in the slip st from previous row,
ch 3, dc in next 3 sts, *(2 dc, ch 2,
2 dc) in ch-2 space, dc in next 16
sts; repeat from * 2 times, (2 dc,
ch 2, 2 dc) in ch-2 space, dc in nex
12 sts, slip st to top of beginning
ch. Fasten off.

Continued on page 13.

FINISHING

Whipstitch *(Fig. 2a, page 31)*
Squares together with B as in the picture.

Edging

Join B with a slip st right after ch 2 corner, ch 1, sc in next 2 sts, [*ch 3, slip st into first ch of ch 3 (1 picot made), sc in next 2 sts, repeat from * across to ch 2 corner. Work in corner: 1 picot, 2 sc, 1 picot, 2 sc.] Repeat directions in brackets 3 more times, join with slip st to ch 1. Fasten off.

If placemat curls, pin to measurements on a flat, padded surface that is clean and colorfast, using rust proof pins in each picot. Steam block and let dry completely before removing pins.

Afghan

■■□□ EASY

SHOPPING LIST

Yarn Worsted Weight yarn, 3½ oz/100g, 100% acrylic (170 yds/156 m)

- ☐ Color A: 3 Skeins Off White
- ☐ Color B: 1 Skein Light Blue
- ☐ Color C: 1 Skein Medium Blue
- ☐ Color D: 1 Skein Rose
- ☐ Color E: 1 Skein Berry
- ☐ Color F: 1 Skein Light Green
- ☐ Color G: 1 Skein Medium Green
- ☐ Color H: 1 Skein Aqua
- ☐ Color I: 1 Skein Teal
- ☐ Color J: 1 Skein Dusty Rose
- ☐ Color K: 1 Skein Cranberry
- ☐ Color L: 1 Skein Golden Yellow
- ☐ Color M: 1 Skein Orange

Crochet Hook

- ☐ I-9 (5.5 mm) or size needed for gauge

Additional Supplies

- ☐ Yarn needle

SIZE INFORMATION

Size: 35" x 42" (89 cm x 106.5 cm)

GAUGE INFORMATION

One Square = 7" x 7"/ 18 cm x 18 cm

Afghan
Square 1

Make 5

With B, ch 4.

Round 1: Work 11 dc in 4th ch from hook, slip st to top of beginning ch to join, (first 3 skipped chs count as dc) – 12 dc.

Round 2: Ch 3 (counts as dc now and throughout), dc in same space, 2 dc in each dc around, slip st to top of beginning ch – 24 dc. Fasten off.

Round 3: Join C with a slip st in any dc, ch 3, dc in same space, dc in next dc, [2 dc in next dc, dc in next dc] around, slip st to top of beginning ch – 36 dc.

Round 4: Ch 3, dc in same space, dc in next 2 dc, [2 dc in next dc, dc in next 2 dc] around, slip st to top of beginning ch – 48 dc. Fasten off.

Round 5: Join A with a slip st in any dc, ch 3, (dc, ch 2, 2 dc) in same space, *dc in next 2 dc, hdc in next 2 dc, sc in next 3 dc, hdc in next 2 dc, dc in next 2 dc, (2 dc, ch 2, 2 dc) in next dc; repeat from * 3 times, end with dc in next 2 dc, hdc in next 2 dc, sc in next 3 dc, hdc in next 2 dc, dc in next 2 dc, slip st to top of beginning ch.

Round 6: Ch 3, dc in next st, *(2 dc, ch 2, 2 dc) in ch-2 space, dc in next 15 sts; repeat from * 2 times, (2 dc, ch 2, 2 dc) in ch-2 space, dc in next 13 sts, slip st to top of beginning ch. Fasten off.

Square 2

Make 5

Work as for Square 1, beginning and working Rounds 1 and 2 with D, Rounds 3 and 4 with E, and Rounds 5 and 6 with A.

Square 3

Make 5

Work as for Square 1, beginning and working Rounds 1 and 2 with F, Rounds 3 and 4 with G, and Rounds 5 and 6 with A.

Square 4

Make 5

Work as for Square 1, beginning and working Rounds 1 and 2 with H, Rounds 3 and 4 with I, and Rounds 5 and 6 with A.

Square 5

Make 5

Work as for Square 1, beginning and working Rounds 1 and 2 with J, Rounds 3 and 4 with K, and Rounds 5 and 6 with A.

Continued on page 16.

Square 6

Make 5

Work as for Square 1, beginning and working Rounds 1 and 2 with L, Rounds 3 and 4 with M, and Rounds 5 and 6 with A.

FINISHING

Following Assembly Diagram, arrange Squares into afghan, 5 Squares wide by 6 Squares long. Whipstitch *(Fig. 2a, page 31)* Squares together with A.

Edging Round

Join A with a slip st in any ch-2 space, ch 3, dc in each st around, working 4 dc in each ch-2 space at afghan corners, slip st in first st to join. Fasten off.

Weave in ends.

1	5	4	6	3
5	3	2	1	5
1	6	1	5	6
2	4	3	4	2
3	2	4	6	3
6	1	5	4	2

Assembly Diagram

Baby Blanket

■□□ EASY

SIZE INFORMATION

Size: 30" x 37" (76 cm x 94 cm)

GAUGE INFORMATION

One Square = 7" x 7"/ 18 cm x 18cm

Afghan Square 1

Make 3

With B, ch 4.

Round 1: Work 11 dc in 4th ch from hook, slip st to top of beginning ch to join, (first 3 skipped chs count as dc) – 12 dc.

Round 2: Ch 3 (counts as dc now and throughout), dc in same space, 2 dc in each dc around, slip st to top of beginning ch – 24 dc. Fasten off.

Round 3: Join A with a slip st in any dc, ch 3, dc in same space, dc in next dc, [2 dc in next dc, dc in next dc] around, slip st to top of beginning ch – 36 dc.

Round 4: Ch 3, dc in same space, dc in next 2 dc, [2 dc in next dc, dc in next 2 dc] around, slip st to top of beginning ch – 48 dc.

Round 5: Ch 3, (dc, ch 2, 2 dc) in same space, *dc in next 2 dc, hdc in next 2 dc, sc in next 3 dc, hdc in next 2 dc, dc in next 2 dc, (2 dc, ch 2, 2 dc) in next dc; repeat from * 3 times, ending with dc in next 2 dc, hdc in next 2 dc, sc in next 3 dc, hdc in next 2 dc, dc in next 2 dc, slip st to top of beginning ch.

Round 6: Ch 3, dc in next st, *(2 dc, ch 2, 2 dc) in ch-2 space, dc in next 15 sts; repeat from * 2 times, (2 dc, ch 2, 2 dc) in ch-2 space, dc in next 13 sts, slip st to top of beginning ch. Fasten off.

Square 2

Make 3

Work as for Square 1, beginning with C and changing to A on Round 3.

Square 3

Make 3

Work as for Square 1, beginning with D and changing to A on Round 3.

Square 4

Make 4

Work as for Square 1, beginning with E and changing to A on Round 3.

Square 5

Make 3

Work as for Square 1, beginning with F and changing to A on Round 3.

Square 6

Make 4

Work as for Square 1, beginning with G and changing to A on Round 3.

Continued on page 19.

17

FINISHING

Arrange Squares into blanket, 4 squares wide by 5 Squares long. Whipstitch *(Fig. 2a, page 31)* Squares together with A.

Edging

Join A with a slip st in any ch-2 space.

Round 1: Ch 2, hdc in each st around, working 4 hdc in each ch-2 space at blanket corners, slip st in first st to join.

Round 2: Ch 2 (counts as hdc), ch 1, skip 1 st, *hdc, ch 1, skip 1 st; repeat from * around, working hdc, ch 1, hdc in the corner st, ending with slip st to ch 2.

Round 3: Ch 2, hdc in each st and ch around, working 4 hdc in each ch 1 corner. Fasten off.

Weave in ends.

Purse

SHOPPING LIST

Yarn Worsted Weight
yarn, 100% acrylic, 7 oz/198g,
(approx 364 yds/125m)

☐ Color A: 1 Skein Light Blue

☐ Color B: 1 Skein Dark Blue

Crochet Hook

☐ I-9 (5.5 mm) or size needed
  for gauge

Additional Supplies

☐ Yarn needle

SIZE INFORMATION

Size: 16" x 13" (40.5 cm x 33 cm)

GAUGE INFORMATION

One Square = 5½" x 5½"/
14 cm x 14 cm

—— STITCH GUIDE ——

FRONT POST DOUBLE CROCHET

(abbreviated FPdc)

YO, insert hook from front to back
around post of st indicated *(Fig. 1,
page 31)*, YO and pull up a loop
(3 loops on hook), (YO and draw
through 2 loops on hook) twice.
Skip st behind FPdc.

Purse Square

Make 12

With B , ch 4.

Round 1: Work 11 dc in 4th ch from
hook (3 skipped chs count as dc),
join with slip st to top of ch 4 –
12 dc.

Round 2: Ch 3 (counts as dc now
and throughout), work FPdc
around the ch 3 from the previous
row below, *dc in next dc, work
FPdc around the dc from the
previous row below; repeat from *
around, join with a slip st to top of
ch 3 – 24 dc.

Round 3: Ch 3, dc in same st as ch
3, work FPdc around the FPdc from
the previous row, * 2 dc in next dc,
FPdc around the FPdc from the
previous row; repeat from * to end,
join with a slip st to top of ch 3 –
36 dc. Fasten off.

Round 4: Join A with a slip st in
any dc, ch 3, work [1 dc, ch 2, 2 dc]
in same space as ch 3, *dc in next
st, hdc in next 2 sts, sc in next 2
sts, hdc in next 2 sts, dc in next st,
[2 dc, ch 2, 2 dc] in next st; repeat
from * 3 times, ending with dc in
next st, hdc in next 2 sts, sc in next
2 sts, hdc in next 2 sts, dc in next
st, join with slip st to top of ch 3.

Round 5: Ch 3, dc in next st, (2 dc,
ch 2, 2 dc) in ch 2 space, *dc in
next 12 sts, (2 dc, ch 2, 2 dc) in
ch 2 space; repeat from * twice
more, dc in next 10 sts, join with
slip st.

FINISHING

Sew Squares together, 6 for front
and 6 for back.

Top Band

Join A with a slip st at side seam.

Row 1: Ch 2 (counts as hdc), work
hdc in each st around, slip st to top
of ch 2 to join. Turn.
Repeat Row 1, 5 more times.
Fasten off.

Purse Strap

With A, ch 81.

Row 1: Work hdc in second ch from
hook and in each ch across until
you reach the last ch. Work 3 hdc
in last ch – 82 hdc.

Row 2: Working into the back of
each st, hdc in each st to the last
st. Work 3 hdc in last st.

Row 3: Work hdc in each st to the
end, join with a slip st to the first st
of Row 2. Fasten off.

Sew end of Strap to each side of
Purse at side seams.

Pillow

SHOPPING LIST

Yarn Worsted Weight yarn, 3½ oz/100g, 100% acrylic (170 yds/156 m)

- ☐ Color A: 1 Skein Off White
- ☐ Color B: 1 Skein Orange
- ☐ Color C: 1 Skein Brick Red
- ☐ Color D: 1 Skein Cranberry

Crochet Hook

- ☐ I-9 (5.5 mm) or size needed for gauge

Additional Supplies

- ☐ Yarn needle
- ☐ 14" square pillow form

SIZE INFORMATION

Size: 14" x 14" (76 cm x 94 cm)

GAUGE INFORMATION

One Square = 4½" x 4½"/ 11.5 cm x 11.5 cm

— STITCH GUIDE —

FRONT POST DOUBLE CROCHET
(abbreviated FPdc)

YO, insert hook from front to back around post of st indicated *(Fig. 1, page 31)*, YO and pull up a loop (3 loops on hook), (YO and draw through 2 loops on hook) twice. Skip st behind FPdc.

Pillow
Square 1
Make 3

With color B, ch 4.

Round 1: Work 11 dc in 4th ch from hook (3 skipped chs count as dc), join with slip st to top of ch 4 –1 2 dc.

Round 2: Ch 3 (counts as dc now and throughout), work FPdc around the ch 3 from the previous row below, *dc in next dc, work FPdc around the dc from the previous row below; repeat from * around, join with a slip st to top of ch 3 – 24 dc.

Round 3: Ch 3, dc in same st as ch 3, work FPdc around the FPdc from the previous row, *2 dc in next dc, FPdc around the FPdc from the previous row; repeat from * to end, join with slip st to top of ch 3 – 36 dc. Fasten off.

Round 4: Join A with a slip st in any dc, ch 3, work [1 dc, ch 2, 2 dc] in same space as ch 3, *dc in next st, hdc in next 2 sts, sc in next 2 sts, hdc in next 2 sts, dc in next st, [2 dc, ch 2, 2 dc] in next st; repeat from * 3 times, ending with dc in next st, hdc in next 2 sts, sc in next 2 sts, hdc in next 2 sts, dc in next st, join with a slip st to top of ch 3. Fasten off.

Square 2
Make 3

Work the same as Square 1 only using color C on Rounds 1, 2 & 3, color A on Round 4.

Square 3
Make 3

Work the same as Square 1 only using color D on Rounds 1, 2 & 3, color A on Round 4.

Continued on page 25.

Pillow Back

Pillow Back

With A, ch 45.

Row 1: Sc in 2nd ch from hook and each ch across – 44 sc.

Row 2: Ch 2 (counts as hdc), turn, hdc in each st across – 44 hdc. Fasten off.

Row 3: Join C with a slip st and sc in each st across.

Row 4: Ch 2, turn, hdc in each st across. Fasten off.

Row 5: Join B with a slip st and sc in each st across.

Row 6: Ch 2, turn, hdc in each st across. Fasten off.

Row 7: Join D with a slip st and sc in each st across.

Row 8: Ch 2, turn, hdc in each st across.

Repeat these 8 rows 3 more times. Fasten off.

FINISHING

Sew Squares together as in picture. Join A with a slip st and work dc around entire pillow front, working 3 dc in each corner. Fasten off.

Sew the pillow back and front together on 3 sides. Insert pillow form. Sew last seam.

Circles Afghan

◼◼◻◻ **EASY**

SIZE INFORMATION

Size: 36" x 36" (91.5 cm x 91.5 cm)

GAUGE INFORMATION

One Square = 6" x 6"/ 15.25 cm x 15.25 cm

——— STITCH GUIDE ———

FRONT POST DOUBLE CROCHET

(abbreviated FPdc)

YO, insert hook from front to back around post of st indicated (*Fig. 1, page 31*), YO and pull up a loop (3 loops on hook), (YO and draw through 2 loops on hook) twice. Skip st behind FPdc.

Afghan Squares

Make 36

With color A, ch 4.

Round 1: Work 11 dc in 4th ch from hook (3 skipped chs count as dc), join with slip st to top of ch 4 – 12 dc. Fasten off.

Round 2: Join B with a slip st in any dc, ch 3 (counts as dc now and throughout), work FPdc around the ch 3 from the previous round below, *dc in next dc, work FPdc around the dc from the previous round below; repeat from * around, join with a slip st to top of ch 3 – 24 dc.

Round 3: Ch 3, dc in same st as ch 3, dc around the FPdc from the previous round, *2 dc in next dc, dc around the FPdc from the previous round; repeat from * to end, join with a slip st to top of ch 3 – 36 dc. Fasten off.

Round 4: Join A with a slip st in any dc, ch 3, (dc, ch 2, 2 dc) in same st as ch 3, dc in next st, hdc in next 2 sts, sc in next 2 sts, hdc in next 2 sts, dc in next st, *(2 dc, ch 2, 2 dc] in next st, dc in next st, hdc in next 2 sts, sc in next 2 sts, hdc in next 2 sts, dc in next st; repeat from * 2 times more, join with a slip st to top of ch 3 – 48 sts and 4 ch 2 spaces. Fasten off.

Round 5: Join B with a slip st in first ch 2 space, ch 3, (dc, ch 2, 2 dc) in same space, (dc in next st, ch 1, skip next st) twice, dc in next 4 sts, (ch 1, skip next st, dc in next st) twice, *(2 dc, ch 2, 2 dc) in next ch 2 space, (dc in next st, ch 1, skip next st) twice, dc in next 4 sts, (ch 1, skip next st, dc in next st) twice; repeat from * around, join with a slip st to top of ch 3. Fasten off.

FINISHING

Sew Squares together, 6 across and 6 down.

Picot Stitch

Ch 3, slip st into the first ch of the ch 3.

Border

With right side facing, join B with slip st in the corner ch 2 space, sc, *skip 2 sts, (dc, make picot, 2 dc, make picot, 2 dc, make picot, dc) in next stitch, skip 2 sts, sc in next st; repeat from * around, slip st to first sc. Fasten off.

Yarn Information

The items in this leaflet were made using various weight yarns. Any brand of yarn may be used. It is best to refer to the yardage/meters when determining how many skeins to purchase. Remember, to arrive at the finished size, it is the GAUGE/TENSION that is important, not the brand of yarn.

For your convenience, listed below are the yarns used to create our photography models.

Scarf
Red Heart® Soft®
Off White #4601
Grape #3729
Lt Grey Heather #9440

Dishcloth
Coats® Crème de la Crème™
Soft Ecru #0117
Cornflower Blue #0870
Spruce #679

Placemat
Coats® Aunt Lydia's® Fashion #3™
Lime #264
Bridal White #175
Warm Blue #175

Afghan
Vanna's Choice®
Silver Blue #105
Colonial Blue#109
Dusty Rose #140
Wild Berry #141
Fern #171
Sapphire #107
Rose #142
Cranberry #180
Mustard #158
Terracotta #134

Vanna's Choice® Baby
Aqua #102
Sweet Pea #169

Baby Afghan
Vanna's Choice®
White #100,
Mustard #158
Terracotta #134,
Scarlet #113,
Sapphire #107
Raspberry #112

Vanna's Choice® Baby
Sweet Pea #169

Purse
Red Heart® Super Saver®
Country Blue #0382
Soft Navy #0387

Pillow
Vanna's Choice®
Linen #99
Cranberry #180
Brick #133
Terracotta #134

Circles Afghan
Red Heart® Super Saver®
Soft White #0316
Burgundy #0376

General Instructions

ABBREVIATIONS

approx	approximately
ch	chain
cm	centimeter(s)
dc	double crochet
g	gram(s)
hdc	half double crochet
m	meter(s)
mm	millimeters
oz	ounce(s)
sc	single crochet
st(s)	stitch(es)
WS	wrong side
yd(s)	yard(s)

SKILL LEVELS

■□□□ BEGINNER	Projects for first-time crocheters using basic stitches. Minimal shaping.
■■□□ EASY	Projects using yarn with basic stitches, repetitive stitch patterns, simple color changes, and simple shaping and finishing.
■■■□ INTERMEDIATE	Projects using a variety of techniques, such as basic lace patterns or color patterns, mid-level shaping and finishing.
■■■■ EXPERIENCED	Projects with intricate stitch patterns, techniques and dimension, such as non-repeating patterns, multi-color techniques, fine threads, small hooks, detailed shaping and refined finishing.

CROCHET HOOKS

U.S.	B-1	C-2	D-3	E-4	F-5	G-6	H-8	I-9	J-10	K-10½	L-11	M/N-13	N/P-15	P/Q	Q	S
Metric - mm	2.25	2.75	3.25	3.5	3.75	4	5	5.5	6	6.5	8	9	10	15	16	19

YARN WEIGHTS

Yarn Weight Symbol & Names	LACE 0	SUPER FINE 1	FINE 2	LIGHT 3	MEDIUM 4	BULKY 5	SUPER BULKY 6
Type of Yarns in Category	Fingering, 10-count crochet thread	Sock, Fingering Baby	Sport, Baby	DK, Light Worsted	Worsted, Afghan, Aran	Chunky, Craft, Rug	Bulky, Roving
Crochet Gauge* Ranges in Single Crochet to 4" (10 cm)	32-42 double crochets**	21-32 sts	16-20 sts	12-17 sts	11-14 sts	8-11 sts	5-9 sts
Advised Hook Size Range	Steel*** 6,7,8 Regular hook B-1	B-1 to E-4	E-4 to 7	7 to I-9	I-9 to K-10.5	K-10.5 to M-13	M-13 and larger

*GUIDELINES ONLY: The chart above reflects the most commonly used gauges and hook sizes for specific yarn categories.

** Lace weight yarns are usually crocheted on larger-size hooks to create lacy openwork patterns. Accordingly, a gauge range is difficult to determine. Always follow the gauge stated in your pattern.

*** Steel crochet hooks are sized differently from regular hooks–the higher the number the smaller the hook, which is the reverse of regular hook sizing.

POST STITCH

Work around post of stitch indicated, inserting hook in direction of arrow *(Fig. 1)*.

Fig. 1

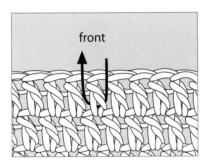

WHIPSTITCH

With **wrong** sides together, sew through both pieces once to secure the beginning of the seam, leaving an ample yarn end to weave in later. Insert the needle from **front** to **back** through both loops on each piece *(Fig. 2a)* or through **inside** loops on each piece *(Fig. 2b)*. Bring the needle around and insert it from **front** to **back** through the next strands on both pieces. Repeat along the edge, being careful to match stitches and rows.

Fig. 2a

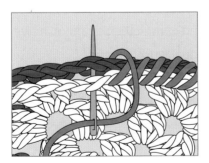

Fig. 2b

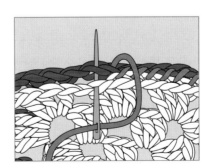

We have made every effort to ensure that these instructions are accurate and complete. We cannot, however, be responsible for human error, typographical mistakes, or variations in individual work.

Production Team: Produced for Leisure Arts, Inc. by Candice Jensen Productions – Editor: Heather Vantress – Layout: Rita Sowins – Technical editing: Peggy Greig – Photography by: Liz Steketee